Finance Tips & Tricks for Property Investors

AUSTRALIAN EDITION

VOLUME 1

First published in 2022

Sherwood Finance Limited
4/129 Kensington High Street
London W8 6BD England

ISBN: 978-0-6454035-6-5 (pbk)

Contents

Introduction

If everything goes to plan, the properties you buy will appreciate over time, and you can use the increased equity as security to make additional investments that could prove far more profitable than the first outlay. Later, we will explore how an investor can use the equity in their occupied home to fund further investments. Better yet, those who build up a diverse and extensive property portfolio will often use a variety of approaches to source capital.

We will outline strategies throughout the following sections and offer our advice to give you the best possible start. It is always worth considering that investors should be cautious with how much debt they take on as their real estate portfolio grows. Regardless of how much opportunity there seems to be, the property market can be volatile, and properties can go through a downturn, which could cause you a variety of issues. Alongside the fact that real estate is not liquid, we will talk more about this in a later chapter.

Most investors will need access to borrowed funds. This may sound like a downside but consider that borrowed money has given countless investors the chance to make a fortune in real estate. Remember that debt against investment is "good debt".

1 How to source finance

When the banking industry deregulated in the 1980s, countless new lenders entered the market, ranging from foreign banks and building societies, increasing investor finance opportunities for anyone looking for loans today. The financial crash in 2008 led smaller banks to join larger ones. As a result, you might not even realise you are working with one of the central banks. On the plus side, new banking licenses have been issued over recent years, although not all of them have gained quite enough traction as they would have hoped.

Another unfortunate truth it's not always easy to get funds for a property – many applicants can waste hours and hours trying to get the ideal loan, only to be turned down at the last hurdle. If you don't want to suffer the same fate, you might be curious about how to pick the ideal lender. We have the information you need, and we will explain it in a later chapter.

While there are hundreds of different mortgages, you could choose from. First, we will go over the fundamentals, covering the type of interest rate (variable or fixed) and whether you want an interest-only or a principal and interest loan.

It is more common for people to take out variable-rate mortgages that last between 25 - 30 years (although may extend to 40 years depending on the applicant age). This is the most popular way, regardless of whether we take the loan out for investment or personal purposes. To clarify this, the interest rate can fluctuate over time based on market movements. This is due to shifts in the economy and monetary policy set by the Reserve Bank of Australia (RBA).

2 Lenders

Mainstream banks

There are four leading banks in Australia, each of which owns several smaller banks and are regulated by federal government entities such as the Australian Securities and Investments Commission (ASIC), Australian Prudential Regulatory Authority (APRA), and the Reserve Bank of Australia. They work by accepting deposits from customers and lending funds to other institutions while earning a profit from the interest rates.

For proven creditworthiness and faster approval timeframes, it is pretty standard for property investors to approach their existing bank seeking finance. Although, on the downside, the bank may not have the sharpest deal or the right policy for your circumstances. There could be another lender with more flexible policies and sharper terms.

Non-bank lending institutions

The deregulation by the Hawke administration paved the way for borrowers to get loans from more than just banking institutions. As a result, far more common to get a loan from non-bank lenders, although one of the most prominent during deregulation was Aussie Home Loans, which rode the trend during the 1990s wave of anti-bank sentiment. These lenders have access to international capital markets and have branches, in many locations operating through intermediaries.

The competition has increased over the years with the rise of challenger banks, providing individuals with specialised lenders with better rates than traditional banks. While limited, compared to the more prominent firms in the industry, many of the older challenger banks have branch networks, while newer ones run via mobile and online services.

We know specialist lenders with great rates and innovative mortgage products. They are more vulnerable to higher wholesale interest rates because of their funding. There is also the problem of wholesale lending markets freezing because of financial conditions, which does not help.

An important consideration is that their mortgage decisions are determined by the borrower's position, allowing them to fund situations that a mainstream bank would not be as willing to consider. In addition, they are open and ready to work with ex-pats and use foreign currencies, a bonus for specific borrowers.

Subprime Lenders

Non-conforming lenders had a spark in the mainstream lending industry. Non-bank lending institutions like Melbourne-based Liberty and La Trobe Financial being examples of pioneers leading this sector. During the late 1990s, these lenders became successful because they filled a gap in the market between private and traditional lenders.

There are many individuals out there who struggle to meet the criteria of most mainstream lending institutes, borrowers who:

▸ They are outside of the typical borrower profile, which can be because of their income, residency, occupation, age, etc.

▸ Are self-employed and do not have the required financial statements

▸ Do not have proof of different sources of income

▸ Have impairments listed on their credit file, whether that's payment defaults or court judgements

▸ Low credit score

These lenders use their method of determining mortgage rates for borrowers, called risk-based pricing, where the interest rate a borrower will be charged will be reflected by the level of risk they pose to the lender. Many would agree that these lenders are essential to the Australian lending market. This is because their terms can often be a better choice for customers who cannot meet mainstream lenders' credit criteria. This could, for example, include self-employed individuals, those with a less than ideal credit record, and customers with irregular income. In most cases, these loans begin with a higher interest rate that will reduce over time (or can be refinanced back to mainstream lenders).

Commercial banks

The market for commercial lending is broad, often being available to a wide variety of businesses, ranging from partnerships to international traders. Whether we need them to start up a new company or refurbish and expand an existing one.

There are various options for commercial lending with the leading banks. In addition, many other companies specialise in offering commercial loans. In most cases, financing will need to be secured against the company's property or assets to protect the lenders should the borrower default on their repayments.

The interest rate is determined by various factors, from the size of the loan to the potential risk the borrower poses. The risk is the most influential aspects that a lender will consider and is assessed by assessing the individual or company's history, business plans, projected income, and much more.

Bridging lenders

Specialist lenders offer bridging loans outside of the standard financing options, often only through a specialised finance broker. This funding can be essential for borrowers who want to move but have not yet sold their current property (or have made the sale, but the funds will not be available by the time of completion for the new property purchase). it's a short-term lending choice that must be repaid when the original property is sold. There are two distinct types of bridging finance which are:

Closed bridging

When a guaranteed buyer for the existing property is available, the borrower will make a suitable plan for repaying the loan by the agreed time based on the funds they will receive through the sale. Mainstream lenders offer them.

Open bridging

While similar, open bridging loans are available for borrowers who have not yet found a buyer for their property. But because of the higher risks involved for lenders, these loans have higher interest rates than closed bridging. As a result, private investors offer them.

It is worth considering what the specialised lenders offer, such as paying off an overdue tax debt or being ideal for investors who need funding for their new project. The large marketplace encourages these lenders to work faster to secure deals to make matters even better for borrowers. Even for those who have unique circumstances, a bridging lender will consider their options and try to figure out the best solution as quickly as possible.

Case study

Bridging loan in Sydney central business district

Property details

In Sydney's central business district and nearby the cobbled streets of the rocks, the real estate was on a historic road, with proximity to major infrastructure and entertainment venues.

What did the client want?

Just days before the settlement date, they refused the buyer finance. He was heading towards legal and financial trouble.

Difficulties along the way

After applying, the lodgement of a hefty court judgment alerted the lender of the borrower's credit file.

Key points

Several specialists are bridging lenders out there, many of which can offer funding outside of the traditional mortgage, only available through the best finance brokers.

What did we do?

We introduced a specialist lender that prides itself on being efficient in quick settlements.

The end results

We settled the transaction one day after the scheduled date. Because we facilitated bridging finance, they incurred increased costs. But the clients understood, and we refinanced them into standard mortgage terms after the court judgment was settled.

3 What is equity release?

In terms of mortgages, the word equity is used to describe the difference between what you owe on your home loan and the property's value.

Real estate investors start off after they have purchased their first home. Since the family home is likely to have gained equity. Maximising your home equity can be one of the best sources of capital growth for property investing.

Equity release is a widespread practice among lenders. Overall, one of the best ways to reduce lending risk. A bank can take out lenders mortgage insurance (LMI) to cover the costs of a borrower defaulting.

Depends on the property's risk profile, a bank may even pay for a third party to value the property instead. The valuer will often describe the house and research what properties with similar attributes have sold. Most banks will have no problem with sharing the valuer's report with the borrowers.

As mentioned earlier, when calculating how much equity a property holds, the amount of debt and the value of a property are the most crucial factors, although it can be reliant on the valuation (which most lenders will need before applying).

It's always important to remember that valuation companies can be more conservative than others. They often have a different outlook on the property market. They need to consider the price that they believe someone could sell the property for.

Case study

Re mortgage on a commercial property in Potts Point

Property details

On a side street in Potts Point, they zoned the property mix use and facilitated short term accommodation.

What did the client want?

The client was an Australian ex-pat, living and working in the UK. They were looking to offer their property security to raise funds for future investments.

Key points:

In the past, many mainstream lenders changed their view on accepting foreign income for servicing calculation.

What did we do?

We worked the scenario with multiple lenders and provided a suitable solution.

Difficulties along the way

The valuation came in lower than expected.

The results

Although the client received less cash out because of the valuation, we achieved a satisfactory result.

First mortgage

In any secured loan, borrowers will need to offer real estate to the bank as security. Mortgages are the most common form of secured lending, with the asset being the residential property. When the home's value rises, people can expect to borrow against the equity in the property. You could, for example, take out another loan (known as a further advance) from your current lender.

Second mortgage

A second mortgage is when a borrower will offer the property as security a second time, while the first lender still has a mortgage secured on it. The first charge will be followed by a second charge.

The first lender will keep the deeds and preside over subsequent charges, so their needs will be prioritised should the borrower default. Because of this, most lenders will only offer second mortgages if there is a significant amount of equity in the property and with much higher interest rates than standard home loans because of the higher risks involved.

4   Interest rates

Each has its pros and cons, and in most cases, with real estate investment, one of the most important considerations is whether a fixed or variable rate will be ideal for your needs.

Many circumstances will help an investor decide on a variable rate loan, such as handling potential interest rates rises. Long-term variable rates work out more economically, but it's always best to consider both options before deciding.

If you want more certainty apply for a fixed rate. A fixed rate will allow you to fit your repayments into your budget without having to worry about any interest fluctuations.

While most lenders have a buffer and review your living expenses before offering finance. When the interest rate increases, the property owners might struggle to meet the requirements of their higher monthly repayments.

> When considering variable rate loans, you may make unlimited contributions to the mortgage. In contrast, fixed-rate repayments are capped per annum, and how much varies with the lender.

Interest-only loans

These are more common with investment purchases, where interest is tax deductible. But one of the major downsides to interest-only financing is that the original capital amount does not reduce, and if the property value declines, they could leave the investors with a negative equity. so, it recommended investors make sure their investment offers capital growth.

Lenders will want both principal and interest repayments on the principal place of residence. Worthy reasons will need an explanation when applying for an interest-only loan.

The offset Account

An offset account, not available with all loans, may prove to be a valuable extra string in your bow. Offset accounts give the borrower the freedom to deposit and save money, as well if linked to your mortgage loan account, it offsets the interest charged on the balance of the loan amount.

For example, with a mortgage loan balance of $500,000 and $40,000 sitting in the offset account over the month, interest is calculated on a loan balance of $460,00 because of the $40,000 sitting in the offset account. Keep in mind the lender charges interest daily on the balance of the loan account, so money going in and out of the offset account will affect the amount of interest saved.

There is only one offset account with a loan package, so attach the offset account to the home loan mortgage to offset the interest charged. There is no benefit to attach an offset account to an investment property loan, as all the interest charged is tax deductible.

5 How do lenders assess investment applications

Lenders will often focus on three factors: person, purpose, and property – known as the three P's. In any situation, there are several things that a lender will need to discuss when assessing potential borrowers:

▶ Which individuals can and cannot borrow in terms of legal barriers

▶ Aside from legal issues, there is whether a lender can offer the applicant a loan

▶ If and how funds should be allocated to separate entities.

▶ What amount should be allocated to each person?

Any good lending policy will need to consider these factors. There are a few examples of matters that need to be assessed.

▶ Market positioning and business levels may affect the lender.

▶ The profit margins they would like from providing a loan

▶ The potential risks that come with lending to the applicant

▶ Arrears, recovery statistics and any other relevant circumstances.

For property investors, its essential to keep a clean credit report. When reviewing your loan, banks and lenders will consider your credit history – and anyone who has applied for finance will have a credit file that will play a huge role in their chances of approval. Debt is a genuine risk that can be hard to overcome, especially for new investors. Even outside of this, one of the most significant roadblocks for beginners is that there can often be little room for negotiation and thousands of loan products out there, so how do you choose the ideal one? A good finance broker can often help with all of this, guiding you through the many lenders, loan options and updates on product changes that could be positive/ negative for an investment.

Most lenders will take your credit score as one of the essential pieces of information during your assessment. They will use your score in several ways to decide the financial risks you present based on your financial history. They will refuse those who do not meet the required criteria.

Other factors lenders consider include:

- Age

- Commitments

- Rental income

- Conduct of bank or loan accounts with the firm

- Income

- Occupation

Most firms will consider these general factors, which, based on their experience, have some bearing on the risk factor of an applicant.

Higher lending charges

When the LVR (Loan to Value Ratio) exceeds 80 per cent of the property value, a lender will impose a fee known as lenders mortgage insurance (LMI) as a single payment (which, in most cases, is added to the total loan).

If a borrower defaults on the mortgage and the property sale does not cover the losses, mortgage insurance protects the lender's investments. The insurance covers the difference between the sale price and the remaining mortgage.

The borrower pays the insurance premiums, but the insurance does not help them, although they may not borrow as much without it. A mortgage insurance contract is made between the insurer and the lender and is not refundable to the borrower. so, even if they buy another property, it cannot be transferred to a new mortgage.

How is self-employed income assessed?

In mortgage applications, public company directors are assessed as employees. In contrast, directors of smaller firms own shares and are assessed as self-employed borrowers. Since the company is owned by shareholders, they can control their income.

It is common for directors to receive smaller salaries. In addition, directors' income can be less stable than an employee. As a result, it can sometimes be harder for company directors to get and sustain a mortgage. Not only that, but when company accounts are constructed to minimise tax (which can be done by showing the least amount of money available for taxation), it does not show the company's financial position, which can cause complications.

The salary of a sole trader or a company is challenging

for the lender's credit team to determine. Financial institutions will use the company's net profit before tax as a base for assessing how much a client can borrow. On a case-by-case basis, depreciation, superannuation contributions and non-reoccurring interest payments can be used for servicing the loan.

Lenders will look for a company dependent on their directors and have security, although they will always check that the individuals entering the contract may do so. It is often best to first make sure that the company in question can borrow for that purpose and be able to borrow enough.

Keep in mind that shareholders are not responsible for the debts of a limited liability company. Instead, their liability is equal to how much they invested in the company's shares, and this is the most they would lose if a company defaulted on their repayments.

6 Products

Self-Managed Super Fund (SMSF)

In the past, SMSFs required investors to have enough cash to buy a property outright (or at least buy with a partner or another party) to get this loan. Since 2007, this is not the case, as SMSFs can borrow to buy the property without having the entire value in cash.

Commercial lenders offer finance via SMSF to buy commercial or residential property. But it is crucial to consider that borrowing in SMSF must be 'limited recourse' (which is why people often call it a limited recourse borrowing arrangement). The lender can only take charge of that asset.

This may not seem so bad for borrowers, but the limited recourse borrowing arrangements (LBRA) introduced in 2009 have had an impact. Most commercial lenders aim to avoid having to deal with the hassle and seek guarantees for the loan so that any members of the corporate trustee of the self-managed super fund will pay the outstanding debts even outside of the LBRA.

It's not as easy as it sounds setting up an SMSF. Several parts of the process include purchasing the trust deed, choosing a trustee (there must be a bank account opened in the trustee's name), detailing an investment strategy, and much more. There is so much more than we have covered in this book. Since a technical endeavour, it's prudent to find an experienced financial advisor and accountant.

If you seek finance for residential or commercial investment by SMSF, remember your lending options are limited, so reach out, support@sherwoodfinance.com.au

---

Low documentation lenders

Self-employed borrowers find it more challenging to get the mortgage they need, because most lenders will need at least two years of financial statements and tax returns to assess. It's difficult to get all this information together and can become outdated.

A low documentation mortgage could be the answer to overcome this situation because this form of financing does not need the standard financial information mentioned earlier. Several lenders will consider a letter from the client's existing accountant to support the borrower's current income. In addition, they will need

the company or sole trader has been registered with an Australian business number (ABN) for at least two years.

The drawback for borrowers is that mortgage insurers do not support low documentation loans, and they have added application fees and higher interest rates.

Case study

The lending bank refuses finance for a self-employed applicant.

Property details

The client was seeking to buy an investment property in the southern coastal areas of Queensland.

What did the client want?

After meeting a representative from his bank, they informed the client that they would use his last two years' financials for servicing and not his current income. so, the client needed a lender to consider his current YTD (Year to date) income rather than his previous year's income

What did we do?

We engaged a low documentation lender, which

enabled his accountant to verify YTD income to support the application.

Key points

Mortgage insurance companies do not support low documentation applications. So, 20 per cent plus government fees are required.

The results

They approved finance; the client was pleased with the outcome.

▸ 80% LVR

▸ 4.29% pa

▸ 25-year term

Construction loans

Property development can come in many forms and use various investment strategies, ranging from extensions to sub-dividing property, all of which will often need further capital after settlement. We will discuss the risks and options in this chapter.

They offer this form of financing interest-only and works as a drawdown loan to fund the project. On larger investments, they capitalise the interest rates during the project's construction. these loans can last anywhere between 9 and 36 months, making them a short-term financing arrangement. But keep in mind that the rates on these loans will often be higher with private lenders, with the costs increasing even higher because of origination fees.

If you consider taking out a loan for your construction project, remember that lenders will need a stable source of income, fixed price building contract, council approved plans, a licensed builder, and a report from a quantity surveyor. In many situations for construction standard interest rates will apply.

> Because of various factors (such as borrowers facing financial difficulties during the building stage of the project, delays in schedule, and many more potential problems), lenders consider these types of loans quite risky.

Risks to consider

It's not a quick and easy process.

With all the time to complete a project, from finding the perfect property to selling it to an investor, several years can pass by. But there is the risk that the property cycle will change, leaving you to deal with the unfamiliar territory where your development isn't as desirable as it would have been when you started.

There may be unforeseen limitations.

It's not uncommon for developers to see their plans fall through because of unexpected setbacks. For example, they may buy a property to subdivide, only to find that the laws have changed and now prevent them from doing so.

Not everyone will approve of your work.

You're likely to have to deal with locals who aren't happy about the fact that you're developing in a particular area, whether they feel the project doesn't fit the landscape or they're opposed to developments.

Which could cause problems with the council.

If that doesn't seem bad enough, consider that they often base local planning laws around local councils and that most councillors will side with residents.

Things might not run as smoothly as you planned

Even the most organised developers are likely to find that their schedule falls somewhere along the lines, and things won't be done based on an original timetable.

Builders can go broke, too.

it's more common than you think for good builders to go broke when the industry or poor business decisions are difficult.

Problems posed by a shifting economy and interest

These projects take time, and a lot can happen, even in a few short years. As a result, the interest rates could increase throughout your development, and the economy could change direction.

it's not always that easy to sell

Regardless of the size or concept of your project, the market is subject to change. By the time everything is done, you could find that you'll have to sell for less than you'd planned. You may even have to rent the property out to earn your money back over time instead.

One of the best things you can do is research everything you need to know, from details on the area to zoning laws. Then, with everything to consider, it's best to talk to a local real estate expert to understand the situation better. Property developers need to have an excellent track record, which is why taking the time to plan everything out and get estimates for all your outgoings can be vital to your overall success.

Case Study

Incomplete construction site in Brisbane -

Property details

A prominent freehold incomplete construction site at a major intersection north of Brisbane was neglected and incomplete because of a shortage of funding from the builder.

Key details

Many lenders will not consider applications for incomplete construction sites because of the added risk.

What did the client want?

The investors saw the opportunity to take

over and complete the construction work, but they needed access to an appropriate lender.

Difficulty along the way

The vendors' insolvency meant working under strict time constraints to complete the transaction.

What did we do?

We arranged for a colleague to inspect and forward a detailed report before submitting a formal loan application to our lender.

The results

We achieved an ideal result for our clients within an unusual lending scenario.

Commercial lending

Due to how crucial finance can be to commercial real estate investments, it's best for investors hoping to get at least a basic understanding, and a professional on their side to help them in making the right decisions.

Corporate borrowing is the term used for when a financial institution lends to a company, whether it's for residential or commercial purposes. Before deciding, lenders must confirm that the company in question can borrow. In most cases, these are not regulated mortgages unless the loan is taken out by a small business and is secured against a residential property.

In a standard regulated mortgage, lenders review the business plan or at least evidence that the loan is intended for business and the decision is often based on the income and outgoings of the applicant, much like with regular loans. The borrowers rely on their business for personal gain and cover their mortgage payments in these instances. In addition, lenders will want to make sure that the company can support the loan costs and other expenditures.

Commercial properties will need to be assessed and valued by an expert. Lenders will choose the lower of their two options (the contract price and valuation) and work backwards from there. Regardless of this, it's always best to consider the securities a lender offers before making any big decisions.

Commercial lending refers to anything not considered residential. Commercial properties can often be defined by higher rental income and growth in their capital value. Here are the key advantages to consider with commercial lending:

▸ You will have access to consistent rental reviews (with a maximum of 5 years between each)

▸ There are longer leases for commercial properties

▸ stable tenants

▸ fewer refurbishment costs

▸ Outgoings paid by the tenants

Potential drawbacks that can come with commercial lending include:

Interest rates are likely to be higher than residential loans. In addition, the cost of the valuation report is higher than a residential property. As a result, the quality of the land and property may not meet the lender's criteria. It's not always easy to find suitable tenants, so prolonged vacancies can be costly.

Case Study

Purchase of a service station in regional New South Wales

Property details

Well located for passing traffic and refuelling, this service station had a long-term lease with a significant supplier.

What did the client want?

Because their existing lender would not increase the leverage on current liabilities, they tasked us with assisting the investor in expanding the loan to value ratio with reasonable terms.

Key points:

Due to specialised security, most lenders reduce the loan to value ratio for service stations.

What did we do?

We searched around for the ideal lender – one that our client had not yet encountered. We introduced a lender that offered perfect terms.

The results

The client was pleased so and formed a strong business relationship.

▸ LVR: 70%

▸ Rate: 4.5%

▸ Term: 3-year commercial bills

7 Structures

Trust Companies

During the crusades, in the 12th Century, the Law of Trusts was first developed. This was necessary because the "common law" was indivisible property like Roman law and civil law before it. The Lord Chancellor had the power to declare who the actual owner was if it seemed unfair to someone with the legal title to keep it over another person.

With the Crusades, when landowners went to fight, they would give temporary ownership of their property to another person to manage – although when they returned, many of those individuals refused to give the property back. There was nothing that a Crusader in this position could do since common law did not recognise this as a legitimate claim. The property and land belonged to the Trustee. Crusaders would petition the king, who would then refer to the Lord Chancellor, and the decision would be made based on his conscience.

In the modern world, a trustee appoints the trust deed to hold an asset for the beneficiaries, according to whatever terms are in the document. However, with larger trusts, trustees will often borrow money for a specific purpose, up to set limits. This could, for example, be when a trustee wants to arrange a mortgage and buy a property – but before that, a lender will want to make sure that the trustee has the power to borrow, since not all trusts grant this privilege.

A unit trust is a modern form of pooled investment made under a trust deed. The unit trust is an opportunity to get a greater return than could have been received elsewhere (with the ability to invest a lump sum of cash into the trust and make regular contributions, or both).

The unit trust companies will only invest in certain shares on the stock exchange and, as a result, differ from most other financial structures since the trustee divides the property into units and allows beneficiaries to subscribe to the units (like shareholders subscribing to a company's shares). Unit trusts offer security and certainty. Since fixed amounts are given to beneficiaries based on how much they hold, making them more appropriate than discretionary trusts. There are other benefits to unit trusts, such as discounts on capital gains tax, assets protection, estate, succession planning and more.

Real estate investment trusts offer their benefits since they are a tax-efficient choice for property investment, allowing private investors to work on a project while avoiding the pitfalls of direct property investments. These are not to be confused with mutual fund operators.

Syndicates

They are used by investors. These funds allow investors to get involved with exceptional quality properties via a property membership. This reduces the risks and offers the best features of property ownership.

This form of investment gives the investor ownership of just one rather than multiple properties, and because of this, syndicates have various members that are unitholders in a private company. It is like a joint venture. A syndicate is a flexible investment choice, as unitholders can have over one project and are not required to be there at the end of the development phase.

Another benefit is that they can reinvest profits. It can be an intelligent choice when considering the potential for higher returns on collective assets. A unitholder can sell their shares to other members (or new members) if they wish.

In the right situations, a syndicate can give an investor the chance to put their money into a fantastic property without the hassle that comes with full ownership or to invest in a large-scale commercial project that may not have been possible under other circumstances. Here are the attractive features. First, investors can buy higher value properties with reduced capital. A syndicate gives investors the ability to spread the risk over multiple properties. Third, by diversifying your assets, you can have more stable returns and reduce volatility. A suitable investment could allow you to get more out of it for less effort and save time in other ways. While several advantages, a few downsides that you should know, such as:

Because there are multiple investors, you will not have complete control when deciding about the development.

There are several considerations for the other investors, from their monetary interests to their goals with the development. As a result, they may hide their intentions or change them later than their original objectives and financial situations vary.

Like with real estate and other forms of investment, there are still a few economic situations that can pose a risk to your project, like fluctuations in the property market.

Joint Venture Agreements

One of the many available methods of getting funding for development is joint ventures. The way joint ventures work is where an investor or lender enters a partnership with a developer and funds the project (from purchasing the land to other requirements) for a share of the profits down the line. The lenders take a hands-on approach and might sign a contract with the developer, buy the land, and earn a percentage of the profits. It's appealing to enter a joint venture with a developer. This funding takes many forms, but is often dictated by the project at hand.

In either scenario, the basic premise remains; a developer and a lender come together, one offering an idea and the skill to execute it and the other with the cash to fund the said idea. Two people come together, each with something different to offer, to run a single project and contribute in their way (whether through the development work itself or via funds).

This funding involves two or more people buying a property. They could be business partners or friends and family, entering a long-term arrangement with other individuals – which must be made clear to all parties at the beginning. It can be vital for the terms of the agreement to be examined and agreed to in writing to prevent any legal complications from occurring later. if things don't go as planned, you must have an exit strategy. After all, a person's situation, finances, and personal circumstances can vary over time or even throughout a short period, like a year.

It could be worthwhile to set up a separate loan for each buyer if you are able. Here, if one borrower defaults on the loan and cannot make their repayments, it will not influence your credit history or borrowing capacity. Plus, even if the loan runs on both ends, separating them can be beneficial in other ways, like counting against loan services (where the lender collects unpaid interest, principal, etc.), which would not be the case without separate loans, as the entire debt would count even though there's somebody else paying a part of it. You may choose to invest with a group of people, and if so, everybody must agree on how the development will be treated and a workable exit strategy. It's essential that all individuals have the same goals in mind, a few of which can include:

▸ If either you intend to keep or sell the development.

▸ Try to keep a modest LVR (Loan to Value Ratio) to boost cash flow.

▸ Consider if you want to refinance or continue to pay off the current loan.

▸ Do all parties involved want to earn a higher short term cash flow or add capital value?

In these types of loans, an investor will first assess the potential risks and liabilities of any parties involved. It is always important to consider whom you are going into a joint venture with, as their weaknesses could reduce your chances of getting a loan (or harm your borrowing capacities or interest). On the other side, if they have a better financial history than you, there is also the chance that they could help to improve your borrowing capacity, which could be worth keeping in mind when you are choosing whom to work on your joint ventures.

Companies

If you dig through history, you find that the first company formation dates to the Dutch expeditions to East India and that their methods have been similar since the early 1600s. In that year, they undertook a certificate of incorporation for record-keeping. They went public, which allowed them to raise a high number of guilders (around 6.5 million) to help divide the risks of their expeditions and allow local investors to earn a profit.

In mortgage applications, public company directors are assessed as employees. Directors of smaller firms are sometimes given ownership of a set percentage of the shares and are treated as self-employed individuals in most cases. Since shareholders own the company, they can control how much they are paid and distribute the profits. They will still receive the same pay and documentation as any other employees would.

It is common for directors to arrange their income to receive smaller salaries, and alongside the fact that it can be less stable than that of a regular employee, it can be more challenging for many company directors to get and sustain a mortgage. Not only that, but when company accounts are constructed to minimise tax (which can be done by showing the least amount of money available for taxation), it does not reflect the company's financial position, which can also cause complications.

Many investors choose to utilise a Special Purpose Vehicle (SPV), a business entity with a particular limited purpose and leave the company's directors obligated to guarantee the loan. The company will be registered as the property's legal owner, and the directors will make sure that all the responsibilities of a limited company are met. Those who would otherwise have taken ownership of the property instead become the company's shareholders, meaning that they own the company and not the property. The restrictions and limits imposed on special purpose vehicles will often depend on the situation and whether the individual can commit the company to borrow.

A financial institution will only lend to a small company if the directors and shareholders agree to settle the debt should the company not meet the predetermined requirements for repayment. But quite a few advantages can come with buying under a company structure, from planning tax through dividends to the higher level of asset protection outside of the company.

It's also important to consider that lenders will often pay close attention to the security on offer, the directors, and that those entering the contract may do so. Because of this, anyone hoping to get financing for their company should first find out if and what they'll be allowed to borrow (as well as other factors that could affect an investor's decision, like a poor credit score).

The setup costs can be higher with most company structures. Many businesses are not eligible for a discount on capital gains (often only available to trusts or individuals), costing them even more cash. Sometimes, companies cannot distribute their losses, making this structure unsuitable. Alongside this, even if a company director is not considered liable for the business's debts, they will still be held accountable for other responsibilities, like ensuring solvent trading.

> Many companies tax advisors have referred their clients, and with our extensive network of lenders, we could source terms that the borrowers and their tax advisors were satisfied with.

Partnerships

In simple terms, a partnership is an agreement where two or more individuals are operating a business together. Unlike a company, a partnership is not considered a separate legal entity and so, all partners own the assets and handle any liabilities. It is always best for a partnership to have their agreement in writing, which should detail all the essential aspects of the relationship, from the proportions of profits they share, to how the company will be handled should one partner leave. Those with a major significant deal in mind may want to find partners for several reasons, including diversification and reduced risks. Alongside this, more investors can also offer more financial resources – and the extra assets could be put to practical use.

A partner might be one of the best decisions you could make for your business, and it could also be one of the worst – although the boosted pool of cash can be handy for those starting in real estate. If you find a partner that complements your skills, you could make the most of the agreement.

You must get an excellent lawyer to create a contract that specifies what will happen should one partner want to leave the arrangement. a buy/sell agreement is the best choice, since it outlines all the terms and conditions for redistributing assets and should allow one member to leave.

There are so many factors that can change a person's life, from moving home to getting divorced, that could cause strain on the partnership. Arguments can ensue when one party leaves, so having an agreement already in place can be vital to protect everybody's interests.

It could also be worth remembering that partnership disputes will only line the pockets of lawyers and accountants and that the business or owners will not help, so there is no advantage to avoiding a legal agreement.

Many people consider family members to be an excellent choice for a partnership – and although it sounds good in principle, sometimes disputes can occur, especially when a partner involves family members with different goals and plans for the project. So, to make sure clarify and get the arrangement you are making in writing like anyone else.

8   Securities

Vacant land

One of the most common forms of property investment available for development is commercial or residential vacant land. Before you start negotiations, it is vital to know the potential of the land by contacting the local council. After receiving approval from the local council for redevelopment of subdivisions, the investor can resell multiple individual subdivided blocks.

Redevelop or renovate?

An older property may appear to be sound. but the outdated interior may need renovation. There is a difference between redeveloping and renovating. Redevelopments are more significant projects that need far more work, since renovations refer to refurbishing the property's interior, such as updating the kitchen or bathrooms.

Metropolitan property

Australia is well known for its size and small population, concentrated in metropolitan areas. The foremost real estate investment opportunities are in mainland capital cities. In comparison, there are many real estate opportunities around the country regions. It is wise to consider that most of the population is in metropolitan locations.

Many experts can offer advice on where to buy; although many suggest inner city, others might instead encourage you to consider coastal properties. But wise to believe that employment opportunities are far more significant in metropolitan areas.

Money can indeed be made from properties across the region, but consider the risk factors that different areas may pose. Even then, nothing is for sure.

Inner-city

An inner-city is considered a small distance from the central business district of a significant capital – Sydney, Melbourne, Perth, Brisbane, or Adelaide.

Of course, there is the fact that inner-city properties are often the most expensive due to supply and demand. but, there are fewer to be found, but the ones in these areas offer benefits like entertainment options and public transport, which people are prepared to pay more for. In addition, living in inner cities reduces travel times and makes it easier to get to work or schools, which, alongside the low supply and high demand, offers better choices for investment potential.

With these features in mind, the costs are higher in the city, compared to suburbs that are further afield. As a result, investors that purchase from these locations help from a robust rental market opportunity.

.Suburban areas

While attractive, city life is not for everyone, and many cannot afford it. There are fewer appealing factors to some individuals, from the noise to traffic. Things like the safety of children and pets (and even yourself) are also important considerations. A substantial portion of people will choose to live in the suburbs, which can be a worthwhile consideration when investing in a property.

In Australia, most residents live outside the central business district. When venturing into the outer suburbs, most houses are on larger blocks than apartments and lower rent than inner cities. The most appealing aspect of suburban properties can be the size of the land, which makes for a fantastic opportunity for property investors (subdivision).

Regional areas

The less diverse economy of these locations is likely to reduce the potential for investment properties, although some excellent opportunities can offer incredible results if you are fortunate enough to find them.

There's no doubt many investors are keen on regional locations. Lower prices can be a far more affordable option, and the potential for positive cash flow is appealing. In most cases, though, it's more rewarding to find a property with a better location, facilities and amenities for the highest possible yields.

Office space

It is common for entire office buildings to be purchased by large investment firms, although they are not as available to individual investors. There can be various crucial factors to consider, like the interior layout and access for those with disabilities. many large office buildings today also contain a café and have most necessities within close distance, which are desirable for tenants.

Office space is considered a category of commercial property. Although not to be confused with retail space, office space can often be renovated and requires a little cost to fit out compared to other commercial securities. This often makes them an excellent base for those who need a collaborative work environment. A lease will last for three to five years, with a tenant paying for all the outgoings.

Industrial property

While industrial real estate is not as appealing to view as residential property, it can be one of the most reliable investment options. One particular help is that when letting on a net lease basis (which most industrial properties do), you will not have to worry about most or all the ongoing costs since the tenants will cover these. The outgoings can vary from one property to another.

When in the right location, industrial properties can thrive even if they have little going for them in their appearance. If there are service regions and accessibility to public transportation, they can still be desirable.

When investing, always consider that certain areas are better for industrial needs. From proximity to shipping locations to nearby freeways and highways, these can be essential, especially for industrial real estate and the businesses using the space. In addition, consider internal roof height, vehicle access, fire protection and anything else that can prove beneficial. We would also suggest other aspects that can be forgotten like floor thickness, the potential for airborne products and electrical capacity, as just a few more examples.

9 Auction or Private treaty

A good auction can be exciting, whether it is in-house or even held on a suburban street. It can become so intense that the bids can sometimes go beyond what was expected because of popular demand. The aim of an auction is to create a large, exciting atmosphere for a sale while also providing bidders and sellers with transparency.

When considering bidding at an auction, it's essential that you first set yourself a budget (and a firm limit) before consulting your solicitor or accountant. If you have any enquiries, contact our team.

If an auction does not meet the vendor's expectations and the last bid is declared to be insufficient by the vendor, the property will often be passed on to the highest bidder or will be reverted to a private treaty sale. The same goes for other situations, too, like if there are no genuine bidders.

If there are several under-bidders, the sale will be passed in, and the highest bidder will have a private conversation about the vendor's reserve level. Agents are likely to tell everyone involved that there is still a chance to take the property for a higher bid, although the first bidder is given the first right of refusal. If they're not satisfied with the reserve price, the agents can continue negotiations with under-bidders.

Auction or private treaty often comes down to producing the best results. In some circumstances, auctions can seem like the best solution, where several investors will be prepared to outdo each other to get the property regardless of the extra money they are investing.

Many homes are sold by private treaties in Australia. Vendors (sellers) decide the price at which they market their properties for sale under this process. If the buyer is not happy with the price, they begin negotiations by offering a lower one.

Negotiation is a natural part of buying or selling a property by private treaty. To get the highest price, a seller often looks for a private treaty sale to work like a slow-motion auction, i.e., offers come in and move back and forth between the seller and purchaser. Rather than taking place during a one half-hour auction with other bidders in front of the property, this may take place over hours, and sometimes days, weeks, or even months.

A seller's agent receives the offer. When a vendor agrees to a request, they will ask the agent to accept it, and contracts are then written and exchanged. A private treaty can seem less stressful and more straightforward compared to an auction sale or purchase. keep in mind that a private treaty requires more negotiation skills from the seller.

Some states need you make an offer in writing, often by filling out a form and signing it. For example, you can put in a verbal offer in New South Wales, Queensland, Victoria, and the Northern Territory and the ACT (Australian Capital Territory), if they are in writing offers are taken more seriously.

We suggest following the procedure set out in your state or territory. If the vendor agrees to your offer and any conditions you set, you both sign and exchange the contract document, making the agreement binding. but consider the following explanations as a guide because local governments and buyers often scrutinise the auction process, and the process could change.

It's common for real estate investors to look for properties without considering the ability of the professionals that could make all the difference to their project. but there are several reasons hiring a team of experienced individuals can be essential before property hunting, most of which will relate to either preventing you from making regrettable decisions or finding the best possible deals.

It's a good idea to make an unconditional offer to buy a property without first consulting your finance broker or lender and other vital experts within your financial team. A solicitor reviewing any legal documentation prevents unforeseen circumstances.

In complex legal transfers, like conveyancing, where the process is far from simple, everything must be taken care of, from paying off all the tax duties to ensuring that all the legal checks have been completed. so, it is often best to contact a solicitor experienced in the field to help you throughout the process.

> Should you need an expert on your side when beginning your investment journey, and before you consider making any offers on real estate, we have an extensive network of industry professionals across the country such as accountants, lawyers and real estate agents that you will help.

Victoria

Auction

At the start of the auction, there is no requirement to register your intent to bid, unless a condition imposed by the real estate agency. Only the auctioneer may make a vendor bid, and they must announce a 'vendor bid.' If a co-owner intends to bid, the auctioneer must disclose this at the commencement of the auction Bidders can ask during the auction if the property is 'on the market.' Dummy bids are prohibited by law. For mortgagee sales, Deceased estates or Family Law Matters, the property must go to auction; therefore, the agent cannot convey offers prior to the auction date.

Private treaty

Unless instructed otherwise all offers must be in writing by the vendor. Besides written submissions, buyers can also make verbal offers, submit a completed contract of sale, and offer a deposit. After the vendor accepts your offer, it becomes binding only when you and the vendor exchange contracts, and a deposit (10%) is accounted for.

Tasmania

Auction

Have your finance and deposit ready on the day is essential. Vendors may bid up to the reserve price, and the auctioneer must state vendor bids to potential buyers assembled at the auction. If the offers do not reach the reserve, you may negotiate with the vendor afterwards and settle on a negotiated price. On the day contracts of Sale are signed and exchanged. Dummy bidding is prohibited.

Private treaty

To make an offer, buyers should use the law society contract of sale provided by their agent. If you wish, you can ask your attorney or conveyancer to prepare the offer document for you. The agent must pass on all offers but may not if the request is below the vendor's stipulated amount. They do not require sellers to show known defects with the property. A cooling-off period of three days. But if both parties choose not to use it, no cooling-off period applies. Once the contract of sale is signed by both parties and exchanged, finance proceeds.

New South Wales

Auction

To take part or bid at a residential auction, potential buyers must register by showing identification and will be given a bidder's number. The auctioneer oversees the bidding process. The vendor sets the reserve price before the auction and is entitled to one vendor bid. If they do not meet the reserve price, the highest bidder is asked to negotiate with the sales agent. Unless agreed before the auction, a ten per cent deposit is required at the fall of the hammer. Ensure finances are ready as contracts will be exchanged on the day. Dummy bids are illegal.

Private treaty

Offers can be verbal or in writing. Although making a formal offer, the vendor is more likely to accept. When the vendor accepts your request, a five-day cooling-off period begins. The buyers and sellers are not bound until signed contracts are exchanged. Then titles are prepared, loan documentation is returned signed, and settlement can be completed. This takes between 30 two 90 days The buyer is required to pay a deposit.

Australian Capital Territory

Auction

You must register to bid by providing the real estate agent at the auction with proof of your identity, and a bidder's number will be assigned to you. The agent can make one vendor bid on behalf of the vendor and must be stated as a vendor bid. The highest bidder must exceed the reserve price set before the auction begins. If the reserve is not met, the highest bidder will negotiate with the sales agent. The highest bidder will have to sign contracts and pay the agreed deposit on the day. Finance must be in place to meet settlement under absolute terms, and 'dummy bidding' is prohibited.

Private treaty

Agents must notify the vendor of all offers and must be in writing. The advertised price must be similar and close to what the seller will accept. The seller can receive offers from other interested parties until contracts are exchanged. After accepting the offer, the sales agent will send the contract and offer documentation to the buyer's solicitor. Once the buyer and seller have both signed and exchanged the contract, it becomes binding. The five-day cooling-off period can only be waived or amended with signed approval from the vendor.

Western Australia

Auction

Auctions are not as common in Western Australia as in other states. The auctioneer starts by detailing the benefits of the property and any relevant information and restrictions on the title. In addition, the required deposit to be paid must be disclosed before commencing. The auctioneer then calls for or announces an opening bid, below the reserve price. Offers from vendors are permitted. It must be specified in the auction form whether the seller will make bids and how many. On the fall of the hammer, the agreed deposit will be paid. Contracts exchanged on the day. Dummy bids are illegal.

Private treaty

If you suggest making an offer, buyers must fill out and sign an offer and acceptance contract (O & A). The agent will prepare either of the two forms, Contract for Sale of Land and General Conditions or the Strata Title, and the agent will present the offer to the vendor. The vendor may either accept or counter the offer by amending the O & A or reject it, and the agent must inform the purchaser. Once the offer is accepted, the settlement must occur within the agreed timeframe.

Queensland

Auction

Before the auction begins, you must register with the auctioneer. A number paddle is provided. Until the reserve price, vendor bids can be accepted, provided the auctioneer announces them in the conditions of sale at the beginning of the auction. Auctioneers cannot engage in dummy bidding or take false bids. After the auction, contracts are signed, and a five to ten per cent deposit is paid.

Private treaty

Agents can list prices over the least amount the vendor will accept. Agents are prohibited from listing below the vendors' minimum price, often considered bait advertising, which is an offence. Verbal offers can be made, and all written offers must be sent to the vendor. When your offer is accepted, the agent must give you a contract of sale, accompanied by a warning statement. The purchaser will need to pay a deposit after the five-day cooling-off period. This takes between 30 - 90 days for settlement.

South Australia

Auction

You must register by providing your identification to the agent conducting the sale. For someone else to bid on your behalf, you will need to give proof of your identity plus a signed authorisation letter. A reserve price is set, in writing, before the auction. You should know the vendor is entitled to three bids. The vendor bids must not exceed the reserve price. The auctioneer must announce each such bid as a 'vendor bid'. If reported throughout the auction, it shows that the vendor's reserve price is not reached. If you are the highest bidder and the reserve price is not met, you can negotiate. At the fall of the hammer, if you are the successful bidder a ten per cent deposit is required. It would be best if you had your finance ready because they exchange contracts on the day. Dummy bids are not allowed.

Private treaty

All offers must be in writing that discloses the seller's name, contact information, the price, the settlement date, and any other conditions. Each submission can include a date by which the offer lapses. Before a vendor accepts an offer, the agent must make sure the vendor has received all written offers. Requests are often subject to building inspection and loan approval or any other conditions by the purchaser or vendor. Both parties must sign a contract of sale before the offer is binding. To complete the settlement, it can take from 30 to 90 days.

Northern Territory

Auction

On the day, the auctioneer will detail the terms and conditions of the auction process and then call for bids on the property. All bidders must register by showing identification. The Auctioneers must not engage in conduct that is fraudulent or misleading. Dummy bids are prohibited. Before the auction, the vendor will set a 'reserve price', and the property will be passed in unless the bidding reaches that point. An auctioneer will often advise the attendees that the property is 'on the market', showing it has passed the reserve price and will be sold to the highest bidder. If the reserve is not met, bidders are invited to negotiate to purchase the property with the selling agent. As usual, make sure that finance is ready to meet the agreed settlement date.

Private treaty

An offer on a property should be on a formal contract, although buyers can make verbal offers, and all offers must be sent to the vendor. The vendor is not bound to accept your submission until the contract of sale are exchanged. At the time of the exchange, the purchaser is required to pay a deposit. The settlement process can take from 30 to 90 days.

Settling on your property

In legal and financial coordination, settlement is when the sale can be completed. Settlement of course also means you can move into or rent out your home.

When the contract is exchanged with the vendor on the date specified in the contract of sale, all parties must perform the required legal work. You will also need to schedule for the lender to arrange funding to be available for settlement.

The conveyancer or solicitor arranges for you to sign a document confirming the ownership transfer at least a week before the settlement date. It may be wise to note that your conveyancer or solicitor will notify you a few days before settlement of the exact date and time of the sale going through, and the required funds you are required to provide for settlement to go ahead. Once all of this is complete, you will collect your keys and move on in – you're now the proud owner of a new home!

Some tips. Don't forget to remove all furniture from the property before settlement day. Also make sure there are no surprises, such as broken windows or discarded appliances (even items like brand-new dishwashers can pose issues when buying/selling property). Items left in the property and included in the sale must be documented in the Contract of Sale.

10 Key legal concepts

Getting the proper ownership structure is essential, as it could save you thousands. The correct answer to your situation can depend on a variety of factors. So, it's best to talk with an expert to improve your understanding of the options, and here are two major structures to consider:

Ownership

Joint ownership (partner, friend, family member, etc.)

In most instances, joint ownership will have similar implications to individual ownership, aside from the fact that you need to consider the amount of holding between partners and whether you would prefer joint tenants or tenants in common.

They do not divide the property with joint tenants, and each owner has one hundred per cent ownership over it. Should one of the joint owners die, the other takes legal ownership of the property. The process is automatic and can't be overridden by any other means, for example, a will or the laws of intestacy.

With tenants in common, both owners are considered a single entity and are trustees of the land, although each is still the owner of an agreed interest in the property's equity (which is defined by the owners). If one dies, their share goes to whoever may inherit based on their will or the law of intestacy.

It's important to understand that the words 'tenant' and 'tenancy' don't involve renting the property, but refer to the joint ownership of an asset (of any form, not just property). These terms apply to loans (such as mortgages), and with joint tenants, all borrowers will be responsible for the total debt. Tenants in common are liable for their part of the debt. banks and other lenders will encourage borrowers to get joint mortgages written on a joint tenancy basis.

Wills

As your wealth and assets increase over time, it can become vital for you to write and complete a will. It is common for rewritten wills as circumstances change. As most people know, a will is a declaration of how you want your assets distributed, as well as other matters. For a will to be valid, it must follow these crucial rules.

▸ It must be in writing

▸ Executed correctly in most cases with a lawyer

▸ Executor appointed

If someone dies without a will, they have died intestate, including those who made an invalid will. There is provision for distributing assets, but not all.

Conveyancing

In theory, you do not need a solicitor to handle the legal formalities in a property buy or sell, but no lender will issue a mortgage unless an attorney handles the legal formalities. So, while most buyers use a licensed conveyancer, a solicitor is appointed in most cases.

The term conveyancing refers to the transferral of a property. Depends on the state in Australia you are in, You will need to choose either a solicitor or a specialist firm to take care of the conveyance. Specialist conveyancers are not lawyers, but they can often care for the legal necessities.

A licensed conveyancer must have qualifications and be certified to practise, and is limited to dealing with real estate-related matters, unlike a solicitor.

You should always have a specialist review the contract before attending an auction. They will research any property title issues and review the pre-sale document. but, if you are not sure how to find one, contact us, and we will help you find a trustworthy professional.

Debt and insolvency problems

During insolvency, a person's liabilities exceed their assets, and the borrower cannot meet their financial obligations within a reasonable amount of time. insolvency accountants act on behalf of the client and work with the debtors and creditors. As a result, the insolvency accountant will decide what remaining assets can be distributed to creditors after all deductions have been made, such as the Australian Tax office (tax debt), legal fees, and accounting fees.

Powers of Attorney: What are they?

If an individual is unable to manage their affairs, a power of attorney can be appointed. While some grant attorneys general powers, others restrict them to specific matters. People with certain disabilities cannot appoint attorneys, and a minor cannot appoint another person to act as their legal representative. In addition, the power of attorneys can be helpful if the borrower cannot sign mortgage documents to transfer or go ahead with a property settlement.

11 Insurance

Among property investors, assessing the replacement value of a property is complicated by the uncertain weather in Australia. The two most common causes of property losses are fires and floods.

It's a brilliant idea to keep track of everything you own inside your home. Include everything on the property. Try to keep receipts and photos as much as possible. Have documentation on hand will help you decide the level of protection you need and give you a better idea of what to request from your insurance provider.

Management agents collect rental income, and a percentage of the rent goes towards their fees. The management fees will be somewhere between 5.5 and 8.5 per cent for residential properties. The charge on a commercial property will often be on a similar scale.

Investors should consider these three types of insurance:

▸ Income Protection Insurance

▸ Landlord insurance

▸ Life Insurance

What does a landlord insurance policy cover?

Rent revenue losses

You may suffer losses as a landlord when your tenants cannot pay rent. They may not settle their rent in the short term because of unforeseen circumstances, such as losing a job or becoming ill. When this happens, you may not service your repayments, resulting in a default on your mortgage. You need to know that not all insurance policies cover the full extent of losses.

Property damage

Renters can cause a significant amount of damage to your property, which puts you at risk. Insurance claims for property damage are quite common among investors. Your landlord insurance will cover any damage your tenant causes, malicious or accidental.

Water damage

Property investors often claim water damage. Water damage can either be gradual or sudden. Examples include corrosion of pipes, leaking taps, cracks in the foundation and damaged roof tiles. Sudden water damage can occur when a pipe bursts and leaking water damages your property.

Theft

Your landlord insurance will cover any theft or burglary losses. for furnished properties.

How much will your landlord insurance cost?

The cost of a landlord's insurance is an important consideration. As with any insurance policy, the rates are determined by location, risk of natural disasters and crime rates. Charges vary based on renting a furnished or unfurnished property.

Will your tenants be able to have pets?

Pets are a significant risk to residential properties. Dogs chewing on doors and cats scratching on walls can cause damage that requires you to spend some money to repair. Your landlord insurance should cover damage caused by pets, so ask your provider. The tenant may need a dog for security on commercial or industrial properties.

Consider talking to a broker about loan structures when you have a few properties in mind to buy or in your portfolio. With all the intricacies of investment, it's essential to find someone you can trust. Not all mortgage brokers are experienced in property investment as you would like.

12 Tax

A Mortgage loan is one of the most significant costs associated with real estate investment for most investors. Unless you purchased the property for cash or have owned it for a long time, you will pay more interest in the early years of the loan. so, a property's first few years of ownership will prove expensive.

Investors may benefit from tax deductions differently, but most business owners find the tax benefit of property ownership beneficial.

The capital gains exclusion for the principal place of residence offers generous tax savings for even novice investors. In addition, vendors who sell their homes are exempt from paying capital gains tax on the profit they generate. Your home can be renovated and sold for a profit, as many times as you like throughout your lifetime. Just remember that serial home selling can generate significant tax-free earnings for investors who live in the property while being renovated.

However, capital gains taxes cannot be avoided by real estate investors. CGT (Capital Gains Tax) is due when beneficial ownership of an investment property changes.

If you own an asset for over 12 months, you get to halve the amount of capital gain for tax.

If it is an interest-only loan you can deduct the payment for your property. But, if you repay the loan principal, there is no interest deduction benefit. Keep in mind you can only claim the interest part of repayments if you have a principal and interest loan.

Currently, there are no restrictions on how much interest you can claim as long as the rent is considered market-based on investments that produce income. Many countries worldwide use negative gearing as a tax strategy. It is not tax avoidance, but the term may mean that for many. Gearing is another way of saying borrowing. When one first owns a property, borrowing is required. Gearing strategies are divided into three types: negative, positive, and neutral – and each class is suitable for different investors.

Accounting becomes more complex, and the record-keeping becomes more critical as you add residential or commercial properties to your portfolio. You will have an even greater need for good management and filing skills if you intend to do all the accounting work yourself.

> Because tax laws are complex, rental property owners should engage an excellent accountant. For instance, certain expenses qualify as operating expenses that can be deducted from your taxable income in the current year. Still, some costs are capital items that are amortised over the estimated useful life of improvements. Consider the following examples.

Negative Gearing

Owning real estate has the advantage of deducting all operating expenses from rental income. Costs of running a business include payroll, maintenance and repairs, body corporate and management fees, utilities, advertising, insurance, land tax and interest on mortgages. You can deduct depreciation from your taxable income, which is noncash but recouped in the next year.

In contrast to routine maintenance and repair, capital items include building and equipment components that extend the useful life of the building or that are brand new. Again, accounting professionals can guide which items can be expensed and which ones must be capitalised.

> Negatively geared assets are those where the costs of holding them outweigh the income they generate. For example, cash-basis investors lose money when their holding costs exceed their income.

Positive gearing

This occurs when a property's income rent exceeds its costs of ownership, the exact opposite of negative gearing. But a property may be positively geared for several reasons.

▸ The income from the property is high.

▸ Rent can increase over time, especially if the property has been renovated to make it more attractive to tenants.

▸ The holding costs of the property are low.

▸ An investor who has owned a property for many years may have paid down the loan to a point where interest repayments are very low.

▸ Interest rates have fallen.

▸ A reduction in interest rates at the Reserve Bank of Australia can cause a decrease in mortgage rates.

Neutral Gearing

Australia cannot produce a property with exact neutral gearing. Such a property would either exist by accident or be a product of engineered accounting. But a property with a surplus income equal to its expenses can be considered neutrally geared. For example, a residential investment property is geared when its after-tax cost equals the income earned from the property. As a result, these properties pay little or no tax. Within a few years, geared properties become positively geared.

In conclusion

If you need information on a wide range of financial products and opportunities, it might be worth getting in touch with a finance broker. A good brokerage has years of experience and will crunch numbers by comparing different loans and recommending a suitable deal for your needs. They interact with lenders on your behalf and they often attempt to assist after work hours.

Over time, the complexity and requirements of the industry have increased, leading to most charging upfront fees. Many lenders have their criteria for assessing applications, and these aren't public knowledge – which can cause some concerns for you when trying to find the right deal. This is where a good finance broker comes in, as they can save you a great deal of time by advising you when to and when not to apply for a loan.

13 Glossary of Terms

Arrangement fees

When lenders charge for the effort of providing financing to a borrower, this fee can vary from one lender to another.

Auction

An auctioneer conducts a sales process in public.

Auctioneer

A profession that oversees the sale of real estate or other items whereby persons become purchasers by competition in public view, the sale favours the highest bidder.

Australian Bureau of Statistics

A federal statutory agency, the Australian Bureau of Statistics (ABS), collects and analyses statistical data and provides evidence-based advice to federal, state and territory governments.

Business activity statements (BAS)

BAS is used to reconciling the tax collected by a business is known as Good and Services Tax (GST), paid to the State government, or annual.

Balance

A statement begins with your last statement's balance, which is the amount you had within your account at the end of the previous report.

Bankruptcy

A legal concept that you would be best to avoid. Also known as Insolvency, this occurs when an individual cannot meet their financial obligations within a reasonable time frame or if their liabilities exceed their assets.

Bid

A method of purchasing real estate at Auction by an offering.

Caveat

A property caveat is a claim to a property as a legal document. Creating a caveat allows both parties to claim their share of interest. Until the caveat is settled, no further transactions can be registered against the title.

Capital Gains Tax

If you sell an asset such as investment property for a profit, you are subject to capital gains tax (CGT). At the end of the fiscal year, they add the capital gain to your income to be taxed..

Cheque

Cheques detail any amount of money that's withdrawn since account holders often write the cheque to pay someone. This includes the number on the cheque and the amount taken out.

Court judgement

If a person cannot repay their creditors, creditors can get a judgment in court.

Commercial tenants

Commercial, industrial, and retail properties are standard in arranging long-term leases. In addition, outgoings are negotiated but passed onto the tenant.

Commitment fee

A fee is added onto a loan to compensate a lender for their commitment to offering to fund.

Company secretary

A secretary responsibility is to circulate agendas and other documents to directors, shareholders, and auditors and record minutes of shareholder and directors' meetings and resolutions.

Contract of sale

An agreement includes the terms and conditions signed, dated and witnessed by all related parties.

Conveyance

When real estate is transferred from one party to another, in real estate, this could be when a seller transfers the ownership of a property to a buyer.

Collateral

Collateral is protection to mitigate the risks involved with lending.

Credit

While this refers to several aspects of lending, most used to describe a contract agreement where an individual receives money and repays the lender by a predetermined date (with an added interest fee).

Credit score

Used by lenders to decide whether to accept funding applications based on the risk associated with the borrower. Also referred to as a credit rating.

Development Approval

Local town planning authorities provide written approval of a project, prepared by the developer's or landowner's consultants, allowing the project to move forward as per the development plan.

Deposit

The amount of money needed to be paid upfront as part of the loan agreement. The amount specified can often vary depending on a variety of circumstances.

Division of Property

Fair distribution, or property division, divides property rights and obligations between divorced or De facto spouses and business partners.

Director

An individual manages a company's operations, with the ability to exercise the business' powers for whatever needs it may have.

Economy

A summary of goods, services produced, distributed and sold within a region or country.

Equity

Property equity is the difference between the remaining debt and the asset's capital value in question.

Exchange of Contracts

When a seller and purchased sign a copy of the sale contract and then exchanges these documents creates a binding agreement for the sale of real estate on agreed terms. The parties are then bound to go ahead to settlement, subject to any cooling-off period that may apply.

First mortgage

When a borrower uses the property as security for the first time as collateral for a loan, as usual, if the mortgage repayments are not met as agreed, the lender can seize the security.

Financial position

An organisation's financial position refers to its assets, liabilities, and equity balances. In a broader sense, the concept can describe the financial condition, which is determined by analysing and comparing its financial statements.

GSA (General Security Agreement)

They register GSA on a National Register to secure the lender's interest against the relevant security entity/asset. As part of the Register, lenders can also negotiate a priority system to make sure that their interests are protected and prioritised.

Guarantor

In property development transactions, lenders could need more security to reduce their risk should the developer default on a loan. This guarantee can take various forms, from cash to property.

Gross Realised Value

In property construction, the Gross Realisation Value is the gross sales (or GST exclusive value of the property) upon the completion of the project. Also known as GRV.

Initial Public Offering

When a company raises capital from public investors by offering shares of a corporation in a public share issuance, often abbreviated to IPO.

Interest rate

The amount of interest charged on a loan, in proportion to the amount borrowed, allows a bank or lender to profit when distributing funds.

Investment property

A real estate purchase intends to earn rental income or capital gain.

Indicative offer

Lenders often show or suggest that the offer may proceed if conditions are met, also known as a conditional offer.

Joint and severally

Where all parties are accountable for the full terms of the agreement, they have entered. For example, in a personal liability case, each party will pursue to repay the entire amount owed.

Land tax

Whether you own or an investment property, you will pay land tax. The amounts vary from state to state.

Lawyer

A lawyer is someone who practices law and deals with legal issues. A lawyer provides legal advice and represents people in court.

Land Banking

Refers to financing secured for the acquisition and holding of developmental sites with no certainty of rapid development.

Legal fees

Upon completing the purchase, the solicitor or conveyancer will charge a fee for the legal work carried out during the purchase process. solicitors charge a flat fee regardless of the property's value.

Letter of Offer

When a lender issues a finance offer to a borrower, it can be accepted or rejected depending on the borrower in question acceptance.

Lease agreements

Lease agreements are made between the property owner and tenant to occupy real estate.

Loan to Value Ratio

All lenders use a Loan to Value Ratio to assess risk when they consider funding and can have a tremendous impact on the terms offered, abbreviated to LTV (loan to values) or LVR (Loan to Value Ratio).

Litigation

When disputes are resolved in court through litigation, unless the parties settle before trial, a judge may make the final decision for the parties in litigation.

Liabilities

Liabilities are obligations between two parties that have not yet been completed or repaid.

Mortgage

A debt passed onto a borrower from a lender secured by a property.

Mortgagee sale

In the event of a default by the mortgagor, the mortgagee claims the security and resells to avoid economic losses.

Mortgagor

A borrower (individual or company) has an interest in a property through a mortgage as security for credit advancement.

Net Realised Value

The asset value realised on the sale is reduced because of standard deductions. so, often abbreviated to NRV.

Non-conforming loans

The term non-conforming loan refers to lending that does not meet the criteria for bank financing.

Non-recourse loan

When a lender can seize the security if a borrower defaults on their payments, the difference from standard scenarios is that the lender cannot get further compensation, even if the collateral covers the total unpaid loan.

Offshore

Ideal for overseas investors, most offshore financing options are available for competitive prices and offer enticing sums of money. The applications to be considered are company borrowers.

Passed in

If the owner's reserve price has not been met, a property is not sold at Auction; therefore, passed in.

Periodic lease

Typical with residential, a tenant continues to rent and occupy the property beyond the expiration of the lease agreement.

Private treaty sale

The terms and conditions of a private sale between a seller and buyer to purchase the real estate vary from state to state.

Presales

A lender will want a certain number of presales to reduce their risks. While the percentage of resold units is not set, funding can vary from one lender to another.

Principal and interest mortgage

A standard mortgage, with the difference that repayments are part capital and part interest.

Property Acquisition

When legal ownership or rights over real estate are transferred, the rules may vary from one state to another.

Property Maintenance

Property owners will need to decide about building works and maintenance. The agent managing your property will manage and looking after the property. This includes marketing your property, collecting rent and fixing any issues.

Progress Payments

As the construction progresses, Lender's drawdown payments in stages. so, the lender needs to report the work completed by its Quantity Surveyor to compare the completed work as part of the loan agreement.

Property Settlement

A legal process facilitated by the legal and financial representatives of the purchaser and the seller. Settlement occurs when ownership is passed from the seller to the buyer. the settlement date is determined in the contract of sale by the vendor.

Profit

When the financial earnings of a business activity exceed the amount needed for the costs, taxes, etc., this could be when a company buys something and sells it for a higher price.

Preferred equity

Investments or loans exceeding the level associated with project and mezzanine debt but not taking part as equal ranking equity are deemed preferred equity.

Rescind

To discontinue a contract of sale.

Reserve Price

The vendor agrees upon the minimum acceptable price before the Auction.

Residential tenants

In most cases, residential leases last for one year; any shorter would be costly for the property owner for re-tenanting costs such as marketing, rental income delays and re-letting fees to the agent.

Recourse

If the debt obligation is not honoured, a lender may seek a borrower's security. A full recourse is when a lender can take more assets to repay the entire unpaid debt.

Receipt

A note any money that is deposited into your account. This is also known as paid-in or credits.

Reserve Bank of Australia

The Australian central bank publishes and controls monetary policy. This can have a varying, underlying effect on mortgage rates.

Settlement Date

The last part of the process is whereby the purchaser completes the payment of the contract price to the seller, and legal possession is transferred to the purchaser.

Share certificates

A share certificate is a document that is issued by a company that sells shares. An investor receives a share certificate upon purchasing a certain number of shares and as a record of ownership.

Stamp duty

All Australian States and Territories impose stamp duty. The amount varies from state to state. Taxes on business purchases differ from taxes on real estate. It arises from the sale or transfer of a wide range of personal and business assets.

Joint tenants

Joint tenancy is the default type of shared ownership. There is no property division between the joint owners; each owns one hundred per cent of the property. Legal ownership of the property passes to the surviving joint owner when a joint owner dies.

Statement of Position

According to their assets and liabilities, companies or individual positions show the current net equity position.

Security

Security on a mortgage is essential because it reduces the risk a lender takes on when providing a loan. Suppose a loan is backed by property, for example. Then, if the borrower defaults on repayments, the lender may seize the property to claim the outstanding debt.

Share certificates

Whenever a company sells shares on the market, it issues shares certificates. As proof of ownership and as a record of the purchase, shares certificates are issued to shareholders.

Shareholders

A person or business that owns a share in a company's stock. They can receive capital gains, take capital losses, and they may receive dividend payments. They are equity owners and have the same benefits and drawbacks as Directors.

Second mortgage

A borrower can offer their real estate as collateral a second time to another lender while the first still has finance secured. As a result, the subsequent lender takes a second charge over the property.

Senior Debt

The registered mortgage holds the property's first ranking for a primary mortgage or principal debt. Developers often prefer senior debt as the margins are lower since banks or significant mortgage funds provide senior debt.

Tax returns

Tax authorities use this process to assess a taxpayer's liability based on their annual income personal circumstances and includes corporate entities.

Tenants in common

A joint ownership arrangement exists when more than one individual owns the same property, but neither has the right of one hundred per cent ownership of the property.

Valuer

A company appointed to conduct the assessment of the current market value of the real estate.

Variation

To change or alter the conditions of the contract of sale.

Valuation

Not to be confused with an appraisal, as a valuation provides a more accurate and recognised property value.

Vendor

In a real estate transaction, a person (s) or entity sells the property.

Quantity Surveyor

A qualified individual that examines costs associated with the building costs. Market conditions impact labour costs and material suppliers with the DA (development approval). Lenders also engage them to make sure that the project is correctly costed.

Yield

An indicator of income by percentage earnt on real estate. It is Calculated by the received net income and the market value of the real estate.

Zoning

The local council planning controls current and future development, including residential, business, and industrial uses.

**For further information
about Sherwood Finance:**

Call us 1800 743 796

head to the website
www.sherwoodfinance.com.au

follow us on Facebook, Instagram
and Twitter.